SOCIAL COGNITIVE HORSE TRAINING

SOCIAL COGNITIVE HORSE TRAINING

Gaby Dufresne-Cyr

Dogue Shop Publishing, Montreal

Copyright © 2026 Dogue Shop Publishing
All rights reserved. No part of this publication may be reproduced, distributed, or transmitted in any form or by any means, including photocopying, recording, or other electronic or mechanical methods, without the prior written permission of the publisher, except in the case of a brief quotation embodied in critical reviews and other non-commercial uses permitted by copyright law. For permission requests, contact Dogue Shop Publishing.

Dufresne-Cyr, Gaby.
Social Cognitive Horse Training.
P77. 13.97X20.32cm (5.5X 8)
ISBN 978-1-997638-09-4
1. Non-fiction. 2. Pets/horses 3. Horse training.
BISAC PET006000
First Edition: 2026
10 09 8 7 6 5 4 3 2 1 / 1
Keywords: horse, horses, training, clicker, social, cognitive, learning, lure-free, attachment.

Dogue Shop Publishing
5055 Bessborough Avenue
Quebec, Canada, H4V 2S2
www.dogueshoppublishing.com

Made in Canada

Before a horse can understand a task,
its senses must understand the situation.

Preface

I ground this book in Social Cognitive Animal Training (SCAT). In SCAT, we regard horses as cognitive participants who develop understanding through sensory processing, social meaning, and choice-based participation.

This is not a system of techniques, and it is not primarily about performance. It is about attention: noticing what the horse perceives, how they interpret it, and how they choose to act within their world. It requires patience, humility, and a willingness to slow down.

Throughout these pages, you will encounter exercises, observations, and reflections designed to cultivate thinking, engaged horses and trainers who respect the tempo of understanding. We measure success not by speed, repetition, or obedience, but by the depth of connection, trust, and clarity of comprehension.

SCAT is an invitation to slow down, observe, and participate thoughtfully. It is a training framework that allows learning to unfold naturally on the horse's terms, as much as your own.

While grounded in Bandura's Social Cognitive Theory (SCT), this book uses SCAT to refer specifically to its applied framework in animal training; the A marks the difference.

The Three Non-Negotiable Conditions of SCAT
1. The horse preserves the option of refusing to contribute or execute a behaviour. Its choice must be real, not symbolic. If the horse cannot refuse to perform a behaviour, cognition is compromised.
   - Withdrawal is permitted without consequence
   - Pauses are interpreted as information
   - Refusal is never framed as resistance or failure

2. Speed or repetition of the behaviour does not evaluate learning. Understanding unfolds on the horse's timeline. If speed is celebrated, performance replaces understanding.
- Delays are expected
- Apparent *nothing happening* is often processing
- Rapid behavioural change is not used as proof of learning

3. The human adapts before the horse is asked to execute a behaviour. Responsibility for clarity lies with the human. If the horse must compensate, the framework has already failed.
- The human changes posture, environment, timing, context, or expectation first
- Confusion is treated as feedback, not error
- The horse is never pushed to *try harder* to compensate for human imprecision

Table of Content

Introduction	1
The Foundation of Social Cognitive Learning Theory	5
The Determinants	9
Attachment Theory	27
Building a SCAT Practice	35
Shifting to SCAT	43
Conclusion	48
Horse Training Definitions	51
References	56
Author Biography	65

Introduction

In this book, I delve into the world of social cognitive learning theory in horse training. The approach transcends the use of food bribes (lures) and overreliance on classical and operant conditioning. Rooted in psychology and grounded in attachment theory (Bowlby & Ainsworth, 1991; Ainsworth, 1979), social cognitive animal training (SCAT) integrates how social animals think, bond, social reference, problem-solve, and learn in different environments.

The goal is to nurture a thinking, problem-solving, decision-making, and emotionally adjusted animal that acts with intention, not mere reaction. SCAT teaches horses to learn how to learn and enjoy the process. By integrating social learning (imitation), cognitive development, and environmental design, we move toward a model of animal training that is deeply humane, ethical, and effective. Nourishing intelligence by using a horse's sensory perception and memory processing encourages consent-based training because the animal establishes its locus of control.

For centuries, negative reinforcement, positive punishment, and luring, has dominated the field of horse training. Behaviourism's two quadrants is a framework the horse views as a direct consequence of human interaction and learned associations. While behaviourism has proven effective in shaping behaviour, it often stops short of addressing *why* the horse exhibits undesirable behaviour. Traditional training omits emotions, internal states, and motivation, considering them as *black boxes*. Behaviourism considers the unobservable processes as methodologically excluded from the external display of the horse's behaviour. Forgoing or misunderstanding conditioned emotional responses directly affects the horse's resilience.

A horse may *walk* on cue, but the emotion driving its

behaviour remains unresolved. Your horse might accept grooming, yet remain hypervigilant in new environments. In both cases, the behaviour is technically correct, but the learner is not truly comfortable and well. When the limbic system overwhelms the mind, the brain goes into a cognitive blackout. When the frontal lobes have a difficult time processing information, the animal cannot learn. The SCAT training model acknowledges emotions are not by-products; they are the root cause of all behaviour. To ignore emotions is to misunderstand the animal entirely.

This is where the social cognitive learning theory excels. From the social cognitive lense, the horse is not just a body responding to stimuli; it is a mind navigating relationships, assessing risk, processing information, and trying to make sense of its environment. Choosing the best solution for an unrecognizable problem is the seat of intelligence. When a horse can decide on the best outcome for itself, it is more likely to make better decisions in the future. SCAT establishes locus of control and consent-based training by allowing the horse to make choices (Bandura, 1977). Negative reinforcement, positive punishment, and luring effectively shut down the decision-making process, creating an insecure form of attachment (Bowlby, 1968; 1988b).

With the social cognitive learning approach, horse training becomes less about controlling behaviour and more about teaching it to use its knowledge to discover and experiment. Understanding motivation and emotion are the key concepts in SCAT. Learning theories such as social cognitivism, constructivism, and situativism allow us to step away from control and toward meaningful connection based on trust. As Steve Martin, the animal trainer, not the actor, says, *"There's a bank between the animal and me; it is called the Trust Bank. My job is to deposit so that one day, if I need to withdraw a large sum, I still have enough trust to reestablish my relationships quickly."*

To achieve such a feat, however, requires an open mind

and understanding that social cognitive learning is not a novel theory. Harlow and his colleagues (Harlow et al., 1965; Harlow & Zimmermann, 1958) demonstrated that a secure attachment leads to a positive learning experience. Without an emotional bond, socially isolated animals suffer mentally and emotionally, often leading to depression and death.

Science established that Ainsworth's Strange Situation Test (SST) is a good indicator of attachment style between humans and horses. However, methodologies often forgo developing experiments that favour foal attachment with the mare in the presence of humans. Some research methods remove the foal for one hour, which increases stress, while other experiments study older horses. The critical period of development in the horse is crucial for its secure attachment. The role of the scientist should be to integrate the diad during the critical phase of social development to facilitate observation and data collection. When we remove the from its mother, it will recognize people as a secure base for its subsequent development. As Schiller says, *"Relationship before horsemanship."*

I am not here to debate horsemanship practices. My goal is to present a new way of training horses that better suits the human-animal bond, favouring safety, compassion, and performance. I propose we move away from control-based training to problem-solving and decision-making, allowing equids the choice to partake in the work we ask them to perform willingly.

Social Cognitive Theory

Canadian psychologist Albert Bandura developed the social cognitive learning theory in the mid-twentieth century, altering the field of developmental psychology. Drawing influence from contemporaries such as Vygotsky, Skinner, Piaget, and later Bowlby, whose work on attachment laid the groundwork for understanding the emotional context of development, Bandura argued people could not reduce learning to behavioural mechanisms of classical and operant conditioning alone.

Bandura's research, most notably the Bobo Doll experiments (Bandura et al. 1961), demonstrated that children observed and reproduced behaviours simply by watching others. He concluded kids were more likely to imitate people with whom they shared a social connection, adding to Bowlby's research on attachment. In this way, observation became a key mechanism of learning, one operated independently from reinforcement.

Bandura's research propelled attachment theory and psychology beyond behaviourism and toward a more integrated understanding of how learning occurs. At its core, SCT positions cognition, emotional regulation, imitation, social interaction, and attachment as central processes through which organisms learn from their environment and one another. Albert Bandura's *reciprocal determinism* posits that factual knowledge, beliefs, feelings, intentions, and environmental influences exist in a continuous, bidirectional exchange. The learner experiences shaping and shapes their world through a continuous feedback loop.

Social cognitive learning theory invites a profound re-examination of animal training practices when applied to teaching social species such as horses. Rather than framing behaviour modification as the result of behaviourism's conditioning processes, SCT recognizes the horse as an active agent, observing, evaluating, and deciding upon its actions based on the behaviour of others. Social animals do not require straightforward exposure to environmental stimuli to learn from it; observational learning allows horses to perceive outcomes and respond adaptively.

The projection, perception, and adaptation cycle finds additional support in the framework of situated learning or *situativism*, which states that learning is most effective when it occurs within the context in which the organism will use the knowledge (Owen, 2004; Durning & Artino, 2011). Think of first responder training. EMT and fire departments organize mock situations in which first responders must rescue volunteers, covered in fake blood and injures, as part of their ongoing training. Situativism asserts that the realism of the environment contributes to the acquisition and retention of information, increasing their performance during real-life crisis.

Situated learning suggests that an attentive observer in a meaningful situation gains knowledge without the use of rewards. For example, if a person witnesses a paramedic performing CPR during a high-stress emergency, they may encode the sequence of actions in the brain's episodic memory, and later recall it, even without prior training. The emotionally salient nature of the social event enhances learning through both affective and cognitive pathways.

We can observe the same phenomenon in domestic species that live in human proximity. Research shows that social animals share a secure attachment when attuned to the behaviour of conspecifics (same species) and familiar heterospecific (other species) (Topál et al., 2005). A horse that observes its caretaker or another equid perform an action like opening a latch is more likely to reproduce the behaviour. Social media displays countless videos of horses leaning to open gates because they watched their human do it. If the relationship is emotionally safe and the environment permissive, the horse is more likely to attempt to replicate the observed behaviour. The presence of trust and emotional safety, concepts rooted in Bandura's theory, encourages self-efficacy (1977).

What distinguishes SCAT from behaviourism is not the use of imitation. It is the foundational premise that animals are capable of problem-solving and decision-making when emotionally grounded. Horses are not merely recipients of external stimulation; they are directly involved in their learning processes. From the learner's perspective, learning and training occur within Bandura's three bi-directional determinants.

The social, cognitive, and environmental elements form a dynamic triad, each influencing and being influenced by the others. Albert Bandur's social determinant includes the interaction between conspecifics or humans, the emotional valence, and attachment quality. The cognitive determinant includes perception, transduction, memory formation, and consolidation. The horse's motivation allows it to project the information it gathered to novel events or situations. Finally, the environmental determinant encompasses the physical setting, such as noise, temperature, and affordances [1] in which the horse lives.

Combining social cognitive learning theory with animal training improves behavioural outcomes and strengthens the interspecies bond. Relationships reframe learning as a collaborative procedure, one that respects the intelligence, agency, and emotional existence of the animal. By acknowledging the complex social and cognitive interplay, we move toward more ethical training practices that reflect the true beauty of learning.

---

[1] What the environment offers an individual.

The consequence of shifting to an inclusive approach improves wellness and the horse's umwelt. Horsemanship is ready for a profound transformation, but it requires a leap of faith. Classical and operant conditioning are no longer revolutions. The real animal training transformation lies in social cognitive learning theory.

The Determinants

Learning does not occur in isolated theories. Horse and other animal trainers believe behaviourism is the only way animals gain new information. However, learning unfolds through a complex combination of social, cognitive, and environmental effects. Attached to the SCT determinants are the horse's sensory awareness, projection, and perceived control. When we acknowledge and nurture an equid's determinants, learning becomes efficient and adaptable. Locus of control transforms into consent-based training. Without a sense of agency, the animal feels anxious and stressed, lowering resilience. Chronically high levels of negative emotions limit learning. If you want your horse athlete to reach peak performance level, you must allow it to experiment and adapt the behaviour.

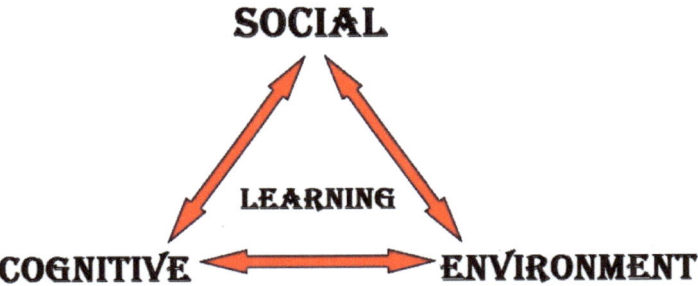

Bandura's social cognitive learning theory model.

Social Determinant

The social determinant of learning is perhaps the most visible, yet misunderstood notion of SCAT. Without a secure attachment, imitation is unlikely to occur. However, once the animal forms a secure attachment, it learns by watching others, whether it be an animal or human performing a behaviour. This process, often referred to as modelling, observational learning, or imitation, requires that the learner pays attention and recognises the relevance of the witnessed behaviour.

Social referencing also plays a major role. Animals often look to other animals and their human companions to gauge the safety or value of an object, place, or action. When the person acts confidently and calmly, the animal is more likely to explore or engage a novel stimulus, the process Bowlby coined secure base. Equine enthusiasts know that to avoid spooky behaviour, one must not look at scary objects. Horse riders repeatedly state, *The horse won't react if you don't*. There's value in that statement.

The quality of the bond between the trainer and the learner is crucial. Attachment theory was first developed by John Bowlby, then joined by Mary Ainsworth, and later explored in animal-human interactions by Adam Miklósi's team at the Budapest University, Hungary. Their research informs us that a secure attachment increases a social species' confidence to explore, learn, and adapt; as a result, secure bonds increase intelligence and resilience.

Horses who trust their caregivers feel safe enough to make mistakes, try new things, and stay engaged in the learning process, establishing their locus of control. In contrast, animals with insecure attachments may be anxious, avoidant, or overly dependent, making the training process more difficult. Most reactive horses display an insecure attachment style with their caregiver.

Mirror Neurons

Another crucial element of the social cognitive learning theory is mirror neurons. Mirror neurons are specialized cells located primarily in the supplementary motor area and medial temporal cortex (Kilner & Lemon, 2013). A decade prior, Rizzolatti et al. (1996) discovered imitation cells while studying rhesus monkeys. Scientists concluded that mirror neurons fire when an organism observes and performs an action simultaneously. *"The same brain areas are activated in motion perception and motion production."* (Sutton, 20023).

The ability to learn by doing most likely originated in social species to answer two fundamental questions: what is the behaviour and why perform it. Survival depends on understanding the answer to these questions. Learning occurs when the organism grasps the association between the action and the result (classical conditioning) of when, where, and why it should perform the behaviour (operant conditioning). The benefit of social cognitive learning is that it presents the emotional, intellectual, and environmental perspective.

A consequence of observational learning is empathy. Social animals benefit from mirroring because it allows us and animals to interpret emotional cues. Relating to sadness, joy, or anger helps manage relationships and conflicts within social groups. Understanding a friend or foe's emotional state keeps us alive; it is no wonder then that humans and horses developed empathy to survive. Social animals rely on nonverbal communication to develop.

"These neurons allow us to learn through imitation, impacting everything from language acquisition to emotional development." (Sutton, 2023).

Learning does not happen in a vacuum. While classical and operant conditioning play important roles, they don't fully explain how horses learn. SCT blends experiences, abilities, and environmental stimuli by influencing the horse's perception, sensory input, and agency. At the heart of the social determinant, mirror neurons trigger social referencing, looking to trusted humans or animals to assess safety and the value of behaviour. Secure bonds foster confidence, curiosity, and resilience, whereas insecure attachments often produce fearful or aggressive behaviour.

By mirroring emotions, social animals learned to navigate relationships by responding to the emotional states of others, an ability that, like human language, strengthened to help us survive and thrive in groups.

Practical Application of the Social Determinant

Welcome to this section on the practical application of the social determinant in animal training. In this part, we explore how to harness the power of attachment and imitation to create meaningful learning. Let's dive into how we can put the social determinant into practice and redefine what it means to train through connection.

Physical contact: Start with a simple exercise. I like to touch gently the horse's nose, then place my hand in front of theirs. I wait and repeat until they try making contact, allowing 15 seconds between trials. This time frame aligns with a horse's short-term memory (Hanggi, 2010), so I count Mississippi one, Mississippi two, Mississippi three in my mind, until I reach fifteen, before touching the horse's nose again. Do not give your horse a treat; this is an imitation-based exercise, not classical conditioning.

Don't wrap or cover the entire nose with your hand; most horses don't appreciate having their snouts grasped and held. Mouth and feet are a horse's primary defence mechanisms; they need to trust you before they'll allow full restraint of their nose, mouth, or feet.

Vocalization: I love making sounds and testing them. When your horse vocalizes, try to imitate it as best you can. You might need to practise the sounds before you can use them. I recommend searching the internet for videos of equid vocalizations and practising them in context. I use horse vocalizations to exhibit that I'm trying to understand and communicate. When I express a sound and use it in the right circumstance, the horse lets me know if it was a good choice. Imitation goes a long way in interspecies verbal communication.

Emotional connection: One of my favourite imitations is yawning. According to Brian Hare's Dognition website (www.dognition.com), dogs that yawn within 90 seconds after their human denotes a high likelihood of a secure attachment. I've tried yawning with horses during various phases of training, and it works; eventually, horses start yawning as our attachment forms.

Cognitive Determinant

The cognitive determinant makes this method distinctly mental rather than mechanical. The horse must perceive environmental stimuli (sensory transduction), remember the outcome (retention). Memory formation and recollection are essential to learning because they establish the horse's outcome expectation. Social animal must have the desire to perform (motivation) and be emotionally and physically capable of executing the task (motor replica). These steps are often absent in traditional horse training. In cognitive training, we wait, we observe, and we trust the animal's ability to think the problem through. Decision-making results in agency.

Cognitive function also rests on mirror neurons to make sense of the world. The earlier example of learning CPR in the middle of a crisis established how situativism plays out. The brain watches, absorbs, recalls, and reenacts; it turns its observation into action effortlessly. Information becomes knowledge, and actions transform into experience.

Sensory stimulation aid mirror neurons by transducing the horse's input, triggering all aspects of memory: semantic, episodic, procedural, etc. Cognitive horse training focuses on olfaction, vision, tactile, gustative, and auditory signals to create positive conditioned emotional responses (CERs). In cognitive animal training, we pair a specific sent (olfaction) with a proximity event. For example, when I train a complex behaviour, I place a few drops of lavender on my clothing. The training combined with the scent creates a memorable event. After the session, we send the horse to relax or nap, consolidating the information into memory. When the horse smells lavender in the future, it will retrieve the training memory, increasing its dopamine levels.

Cognitive training includes associative learning through behaviourism, constructivism, and situativism. Teaching the horse simple behaviours, and allowing it to experiment and expand its knowledge, is the guiding principle of learning how to learn. When you enjoy doing something, you want to do it all the time. So do horses. Dopamine and endorphins increase motivation when released during training; thus, we can use this information to our advantage. Training an adult horse using SCAT may take longer at first, but the resulting behaviour is stronger and more flexible when we focus on the natural release of neurochemicals. Foals trained with SCAT, however, learn much faster than the general adult population.

A horse that learns to open a latch by watching another horse is not just imitating; it is problem-solving. Social animals are inferring: *If I do what it* [animal or human] *did, I might get what it got and what I want.* This internalization of learning promotes intelligence by building confidence, which reinforces the desire to engage again. An intelligent horse does not challenge its caregiver out of spite or disobedience; it simply sees a better solution to the problem and solves it. If we truly trust our horses, we have to let them take action because at the heart of consent-based training is the opportunity for the animal to thrive on its own terms.

In the late 19th and early 20th century, Wilhelm von Osten inadvertently trained and toured Germany with his horse, Clever Hans, demonstrating its cognitive abilities. Unaware, von Osten trained Hans to perform mathematics and other complex tasks using cognition and social referencing. The famous equid is a good example of how horses learn without prior training. *"Hans, however, was also a faithful mirror of all the errors of the questioner."* (Pfungst, 1911).

"Hans still remains a phenomenon not only in excelling all his critics in the power of observation, but also in that he is the first of his species, in fact the first animal, in which this extraordinary perceptual power has been proven experimentally to be present." - Pfungst, 1907.

Neurochemistry and neurobiology manage cognition, and studies confirm the effect of dopamine on learning. According to Sapolsky's research on saliva samples during training (2017), dopamine peaks between cue anticipation and crashes once we bridge (click) the behaviour. Dopamine levels slightly increase during the reward phase, but that is another anticipatory response to a conditioned stimulus: the anticipation of a food reward after a click.

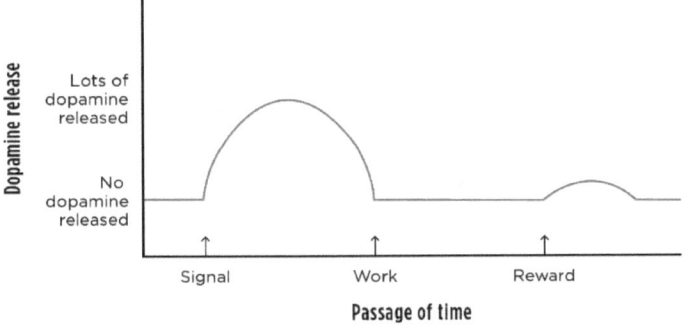

Dopamine release during a training session (Sapolsky, 2017).

The science confirms Sapolsky's research that learning how to learn is more reinforcing than the reward itself, dispelling the idea that animals work for food. Horses work because it makes them feel good; the treat or petting is the paycheck for a job well done. When people use lures (food bribes) the animal does not learn; it is following a food cue. SCAT teaches animals to work despite food because when the task becomes mundane or boring, the food no longer holds value; to avoid this, trainers change the cognitive task.

Behaviourism does not allow for such fluidity between behaviours.

SCAT leans on attention, motivation, and emotional readiness processes often driven by mirror neurons and enriched through sensory perception. While adult horses may take longer to adapt, foals excel under this model, often outpacing their peers. Dopamine, the neurochemical marker of anticipation and effort, peaks during the work phase, not the reward, proving that when horses enjoy the process, they'll return to it willingly. A horse that finds a better way is not being defiant; it is being intelligent. Trusting our horses means stepping back, observing, and giving them the freedom to thrive on their own terms.

Practical Application of the Cognitive Determinant

Training a behaviour: The *Touch* behaviour is a good choice. Grab some treats and stand slightly to one side so you can observe its reaction. Gently approach and place your open palm on the tip of your horse's nose. Be careful not to block the nostrils, as preventing your horse from breathing would quickly destroy trust. Once your hand is on the horse's nose, say *good* [name] and give a treat. Repeat this pairing 10 to 15 times. Then, place your hand two inches away and wait. If your horse anticipates the next step and moves toward your hand, touching it, say, *good horse* or click and reward.

You can download the *Beyond the Lure: Teaching Touch* e-book for the full training protocol. Although originally written for dogs, the protocol applies across social species, including horses. I use these cues during challenging situations. Like mental push-ups, these behaviours, given at random times and intervals, keep horses cognitively focused, helping them from going over threshold and losing emotional control.

Directed brain games: Use its food ration, sweet treats, or regular chopped hay. It is hard to explain how to play a directed brain game without seeing the puzzle or knowing which one you have. The goal is to show the horse the part of the toy you want it to interact with, demonstrate the action, and then invite your horse to solve the problem. If your horse engages with a different section of the toy than the one you designated, stop. I place my hands on the game and say, *Stop!* Don't pull the game away; your horse might think you're taking the fun away. Instead, ask for a *backup* and show the solution again. This game will take much longer when you direct it, but you must follow the rules:

1. The horse cannot quit—ever. Quitting teaches the animal to fail by consolidating the failure.
2. If the game is too hard, make it easier and carry on. You're trying to avoid quitting.
3. Check for treats to ensure the horse is working with purpose. No treats, no game.
4. The game disappears when finished.

Work your way up from easy to advanced puzzles to avoid frustration. If you have multiple horses, you might need to isolate yourself with the player. Horse are notorious for disrupting their mates' brain game sessions because they understand the value of work through imitation. A side effect of directed brain games is fatigue, so they are good for seniors, during recovery or an illness, before turnouts, and on cold or rainy days.

We will see next that over or under stimulation creates behaviour problems, so be creative with your games. My favourite commercial brain games is Kong's green Equine Classic 12 inch Kong with treat Ring. My second favourite Brain Game is the horse silicone snuffle mat, by Excellent. The toy is a slow feeder that you can use as a cognitive puzzle. By directing the horse to the area you want it to eat, you can teach your horse to follow your direction. Commercial games are wonderful for easy-to-clean and on-the-road options.

Silicone horse snuffle mat by Excellent (images © Excellent, 2025)

Environmental Determinant

The environmental determinant is the context in which learning occurs. Horses' surroundings affect how safe they feel. A chaotic or unpredictable environment makes it difficult for the learner to concentrate. Likewise, a space void of stimuli or overly controlled may reduce exploration. I've often heard over the years the quote *"If we can train a lion, we can train horses."* Although the idea that we train horses and lions using the same scientific learning theories is true, the claim is false.

Carrot Ball horse brain game by Shires Equestrian.

Humans entirely regulate the lives of captive animals. We decide when, where, what, and how lions eat, sleep, reproduce, exercise, train, etc. We control stress levels, medical interventions, even death, allowing for little to no margin of error. People highly regulate exotic animal environments. Although we control most of our horse's existence, as soon as they step outside or travel, the environment becomes unpredictable. Even in the structured existence of a stable or farmstead, horses can get into mischief or experience environmental mishaps.

SCAT thrives in enriched environments where horses feel adequately stimulated and secure. The surroundings should offer clear expectations, positive experiences, and various opportunities for learning. Track systems like Paddock Paradise (Jackson, 2013) are a wonderful example of husbandry-based social cognitive adaptation.

Stress-free and stress-prone settings decrease learning,

but SCAT addresses the problem by focusing on building a secure attachment within imperfect environments. The key is to find the balance between eustress, stress, and distress. In polymorphous environments, the social and cognitive determinants can truly flourish. When horses have space to observe, time to process information, and the emotional freedom to attempt behaviours, learning becomes an act of partnership rather than obedience.

As SCAT trainers, our role shifts from controller to facilitator, guiding equids in the direction we choose. The symbiotic partnership develops into a relationship like no other, where learning is not the result of extensive conditioning, but of problem-solving and effective decision-making.

Psychological aspects such as social and cultural beliefs, resources, and access to information shape character. Our lack of control over another's mind directly affects relationships. When we ignore negative, punitive, or forceful interactions and adverse stimuli, we allow those distrusting moments to reshape our horse's behaviour. Over time, these seemingly small incidents can erode the social fabric you've worked so hard to build.

I know firsthand how challenging entitled people can be when they insist on touching your horse. However, the lack of intervention over time causes horses to misbehave because when one determinant fails, learning ceases. It is our responsibility to ensure our horse's safety and wellbeing, even if it means being rude. Reciprocal determinism builds self-efficacy, or the belief in our ability; however, if we ignore withdrawals of trust, we inadvertently deplete our bank account.

Protecting your horse from undesirable interactions is not overreacting; it is safeguarding your investment. When horses lose trust, they stop thinking and start reacting, falling back on aggressive behaviours to solve problems. As horse trainers, it is our responsibility to ensure the animal's surroundings support its growth, because without a reliable connection, learning stagnates and behaviour deteriorates.

Abilities, personal, social, and environmental factors directly influence a horse's confidence. Motivation increases the desire to perform through challenges by attempting new solutions because dopamine spikes during the work phase. However, if trust is low, horses lose trust in people and bite, kick, or bully their way through situations.

The following image describes Bandura's learning model in more detail. The environmental determinant includes positive and negative stimuli combined with stress, distress, and eustress, while cognition includes semantic conditioning, perception, transduction, interpretation, along with memory encoding and decoding. Finaly, the social determinant incorporates attachment, biological function, cultural conditioning, and imitation. If you or the horse needs to urinate during training, the biological need blocks learning.

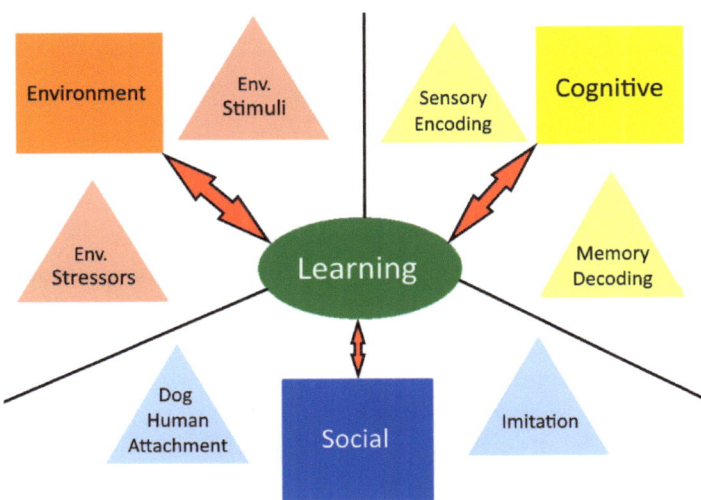

Bandura's social cognitive learning detailed model.

Practical Application of the Environment Determinant

The environment is not merely a backdrop of stimuli; it is an active agent in learning. To train animals using social cognitive methods, we must therefore select and manipulate the environment with intention. We must be hypervigilant and constantly aware of our surroundings to react promptly. As prey animals, horses live in a perpetual state of presence, and once you become conscious of their endless awareness, you realize how exhausting living in the past or future is. Cognition consumes 30% to 40% of the energy we produce; that is why working the mind is gruelling.

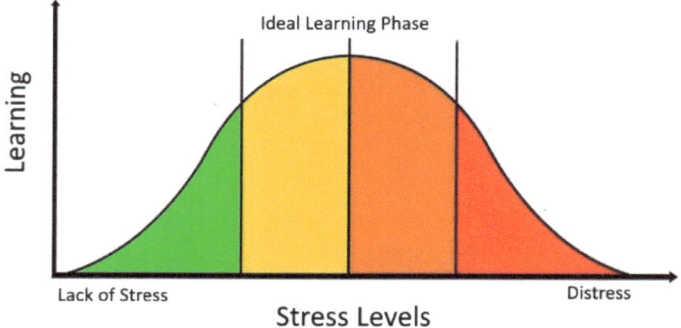

The ideal stress level for learning, according to Sapolsky (2017).

Robert Sapolsky's research on stress offers a useful lens to understand how stress can optimize or inhibit learning. His work shows that learning occurs most effectively under moderate stress, what he calls the *ideal learning zone*, or phase. A horse reaches this state when enough stimulation grabs its attention, but it does not become overwhelmed, shut down (learned helplessness), or act out of survival. High levels of cortisol, typically associated with fear, aggression, or unpredictability, impair memory formation and inhibit social and cognitive functions. Conversely, no challenge at all results in boredom and disengagement.

When applying this to horse training, especially from a social cognitive perspective, the goal is to construct or use environments that produce moderate, manageable stressors which encourage attention. These constructs become the stage for social referencing, observational learning, and desensitization. Social cognitive animal training increases stress levels, overtime, to build resilience.

Desensitizing a reactive horse in public: Traditional approaches use negative reinforcement and positive punishment. These approaches yield the opposite outcome, increasing undesirable behaviour or teaching learned helplessness. We can use the environment itself as the facilitator by selecting real-world situations that promote learning. Let's consider a horse that is reactive on walks or when away from the barn.

Instead of isolating the learner horse (LH), choose a scenario with a naturally calm horse enjoying hay in a paddock. The key here is environmental selection. Do not expose the LH to a reactive or excited horse; instead, choose a context in which the teacher horse (TH) passively models calm behaviour. Encourage the LH to watch, smell, and communicate with the TH without direct interaction. The goal is to enhance social learning by letting the LH witness the TH behaving neutrally or positively. While the LH observes, introduce one behaviour listed on page 34, in a randomized sequence.

Adding cognitive exercises helps horses focus, reducing the likelihood of their emotions going beyond threshold. Think of an EMT or ER doctor asking simple questions like *What's your name? Do you have kids? How old are you?* These questions serve two purposes: 1. It helps assess potential brain damage, and 2. It prevents the patient from going into shock (above emotional threshold) because emotional distress increases the likelihood of death.

To maintain the optimal stress window, we must monitor this arrangement closely; I find an extra pair of eyes helps. We must assess the horse's arousal level before and during the session by determining emotional and cognitive loads. This is a deliberate configuration designed to support social learning.

The aim is to approach the TH without a reaction. Take one step forward. If the LH moves back, acknowledge the retreat. If it moves forward, reinforce its approach, and reward it with scratches, treats, or withdrawal. Horses are social, so satisfying their need for space is rewarding. I offer all three types of rewards, marking the horse's choice with great enthusiasm. Before taking another step forward, ask the LH to *touch* two to three times, moving your hand in different places (left, right, up, down) to keep your horse focused, before reinforcing. The goal is not to interact with the TH; your goal is to teach the LH it has choices: interact, observe, or leave.

Building confidence with terrain: The environment is a confidence-building tool in which insecure horses benefit from navigating uneven, complex topographies that include large boulders, fallen logs, sand pits, pebble paths, and water sources. Think Parkour. Use the four phases of curiosity, look, approach, investigate, interact, and reward the horse when it exhibits the *look* behaviour. I start my training sessions with the *What's This* cue, for it informs the animal which stimulus we are working on.

Don't force the horse; let it problem-solve and decide for itself. The horse must problem-solve how to step up, balance, and descend, learning through trial and error, experience, and encouragement. This physical self-efficacy lays the foundation for locus of control. Again, Sapolsky's ideal stress level applies. A rock that's too high becomes a source of panic; one that's too low becomes boring. Choosing terrain that encourages curiosity but requires effort. When done in a social setting, or with a trainer's calm guidance, the LH internalizes emotional states from others, what social cognitive theory calls vicarious experience.

The role of predictability and choice: To promote predictability and choice, environments should incorporate exits, pauses, and rest zones. The horse should have agency whether to approach, observe from a distance, jump, or circle the obstacle. When a horse hesitates, I encourage investigation and reinforce with a reward. Environments that offer safe autonomy enable learning through exploration, which is central to SCAT.

Harnessing the social, cognitive, and environmental determinants is about more than placing a horse in a field. It is about sculpting the environment to create emotionally safe, cognitively enriching, and socially meaningful opportunities for learning. Using Sapolsky's stress model as a guide, we can design horse training sessions that stimulate without overwhelming, challenge without defeating, and teach without coercion. Whether the goal is desensitization, socialization, or confidence-building, the environment must always be the silent teacher.

Attachment Theory

Social cognitive animal training would be incomplete without a section on attachment theory. At the heart of SCAT lies the relationship between individuals, and in social cognitive learning theory, attachment deeply influences the human-animal bond. Understanding how horses form emotional connections with their caregivers not only enriches our comprehension of social behaviour but also reveals the psychological foundation upon which trust, cooperation, and learning exist. By exploring attachment theory, from its monkey origins to its application in human and equid behaviour, we uncover powerful insights that can transform how we teach, connect with, and care for our horses.

Attachment theory began with John Bowlby, a British psychiatrist whose 1958 papers, *The Nature of the Child's Tie to His Mother, Separation Anxiety,* and *Grief and Mourning in Infancy and Early Childhood,* challenged Freudian models by proposing that infants possess an innate behavioural system aimed at maintaining proximity to caregivers for survival. Drawing on ethology, mainly Konrad Lorenz's imprinting research and Harlow's experiments with rhesus monkeys, Bowlby argued that the mother-infant attachment is an evolutionary adaptation that forms the foundation for secure exploration and emotional development. Building on this, in 1969 Bowlby published *Attachment and Loss: Volume 1 — Attachment,* formally articulating his framework of the secure base and introducing the concept of internal working models that guide future relationships.

Mary Ainsworth, initially mentored by Bowlby at the Tavistock Clinic, enriched the theory through empirical work, including a field study in Uganda and the famed Strange Situation Procedure (SSP). Later, in a cohort of American infants aged 12–18 months, Ainsworth observed distinct behavioural responses to separation and reunion, identifying attachment styles classified as secure, insecure avoidant, and insecure ambivalent, and eventually adding an insecure disorganized style. Her landmark monograph *Patterns of Attachment* codified these four attachment types, showing that maternal sensitivity, accurately perceiving and responding to infant cues, was the strongest predictor of a secure attachment style (Ainsworth, 1978). Inge Bretherton's seminal 1992 review further traced the intellectual lineage from John Bowlby's ethological-psychoanalytic synthesis to Mary Ainsworth's methodological rigour.

Attachment theory, originally developed to understand the emotional bonds between infants and their caregivers. These four styles reflect how an individual copes with stress, seeks comfort, and maintains proximity to a caregiver. The mother's responsiveness, consistency, and sensitivity shape attachment during early social development. After initially studying these styles in rhesus monkeys, researchers have since observed, adapted, and validated them in humans, dogs, and horses, and they show remarkable similarities across species (DeAraugo et al. 2014; Duranton & Gaunet, 2018; Harlow & Zimmermann, 1958; Harlow et al., 1965; Hartmann et al., 2021; Topál et al., 1998).

Secure Attachment Style

A secure attachment develops when the caregiver is reliably responsive, emotionally available, and sensitive to the baby's needs. This fosters trust, emotional regulation, and a strong sense of safety. In human infants, a securely attached child uses the caregiver as a *secure base* from which to explore their environment. In the Strange Situation Procedure (SSP), the child may show mild distress when the caregiver leaves, but the caregiver can easily comfort the child upon his or her return. These children become confident, emotionally balanced, and socially adaptable.

In equids, research is still exploring the human-horse

attachment hypothesis, and the results are promising. The problem lies in the experimental model. Method designs include removing the foal from the mare to socialize and test attachment, or subjecting the mother-baby diad to negative reinforcement training techniques.

Securely attached horses show a preference for their primary caregiver, seek comfort from them when stressed, and return to exploration when comforted. Horse who profited from early human socialization without removal are more likely to handle novel environments, tolerate frustration, and recover quickly from separation. Secure horses typically engage well in training because they trust the human partner and feel safe exploring new tasks.

Insecure-Avoidant Attachment

In this style, the caregiver is emotionally distant, inconsistent, or unresponsive to the individual's emotional cues. The result is an attachment marked by emotional self-sufficiency and suppression of distress.

In human infants, an insecure avoidant attached child may not appear distressed when the caregiver leaves and may actively avoid them upon return. This is not a sign of independence but rather a coping strategy to deal with unresponsive caregiving. These children often struggle to express emotions and may appear emotionally detached.

In equids, avoidant animals may seem well-behaved or independent because they suppress stress signals. Horses may not seek their caregiver when anxious, show little interest in reunion, and avoid social interaction under stress. In training, these horses may appear disengaged, hesitant to try new behaviours, or shut down under pressure. It is easy to mistake this detachment for obedience or calmness, when it often reflects emotional withdrawal. We refer to this process as learned helplessness: the process by which an animal does not know how to respond, thus it becomes emotionally unavailable and can no longer take action.

Insecure-Ambivalent Attachment

This style of attachment forms when caregiving is inconsistent, sometimes responsive, other times rejecting or unpredictable. The child becomes hypervigilant, clingy, and uncertain about whether the caregiver will meet his or her needs. In human infants, these children show intense distress when the caregiver leaves and ambivalent behaviour upon return, seeking contact but also resisting it. They may cry more, cling excessively, and have difficulty being soothed. This pattern stems from the infant's uncertainty about the caregiver's availability and reliability.

In horses, the ambivalent attachment style often looks like clinginess or hyper-attachment. These horses may become extremely distressed during separation, vocalize excessively, or follow their caregiver relentlessly. Upon reunion, they may simultaneously seek contact and display signs of frustration or anxiety. Training such horses can be difficult, as they often focus their attention on the caregiver's availability rather than on the task at hand. They may show inconsistent performance and struggle with independence. People often refer to these horses as *space invaders*: horses that do not understand boundaries.

Disorganized Attachment

Disorganized attachment emerges when the caregiver is both a source of comfort and fear, typically because of neglect, trauma, or abuse, with an increase in dysfunction when all three are present. The resulting behaviour is confused, contradictory, and fearful. Insecure aggression is a common diagnosis among horses who suffer from disorganized attachment.

In human infants, disorganized children exhibit no coherent strategy to cope with separation or stress. They may freeze, display stereotypic movements, or approach the caregiver while looking away. This attachment style is strongly associated with early trauma or severe disruptions in caregiving.

In horses, disorganized attachment can manifest as erratic behaviour, fearfulness, or aggression directed toward the caregiver. These horses may approach and then suddenly retreat, show excessive startle responses, or bite without warning. They often display conflicting signals, such as tail wagging combined with avoidance or growling while seeking proximity. This attachment style is rare in securely raised horses, but we can observe it in animals from abusive or highly chaotic backgrounds. We must approach training with extreme care, patience, and often involves a behaviour professional.

Recognizing attachment in animals helps professionals respond with greater empathy and effectiveness. In horse training, attachment-informed practice fosters deeper trust, better communication, and a safer emotional environment in which horses can learn. By cultivating secure attachments, we are not only improving obedience or skill development; we are supporting the horse's emotional health, social flexibility, and long-term resilience.

Attachment in Horses

In 1998, József Topál, alongside Miklósi, Csányi, and Dóka, extended human attachment theory to horses. Using an adapted SSP, they examined 51 horse–owner pairs and discovered that horses exhibit behaviours analogous to human infants: exploration, separation protest, and secure-base effects. Their analysis revealed distinct attachment styles in horses, including secure and insecure patterns.

Subsequent studies, including a 2019 adaptation of Ainsworth's classification, found that approximately 61% of horses have a secure attachment, a distribution strikingly similar to human infants. These attachment patterns correlated with owner sensitivity, reinforcing the parallel: horses form attachments based on responsive caregiving.

Attachment theory has far-reaching implications for horse training, particularly when we examine the human-horse bond through the lens of emotional security and trust. When a horse forms a secure attachment with its human caregiver, that person becomes a secure base, a concept first articulated by Bowlby and empirically validated by Ainsworth. In practical terms, this means the horse feels safe enough in the caregiver's presence to explore, learn, and recover from stress. In training settings, this secure base dynamic plays a crucial role in how horses process information, manage arousal, and engage with the environment.

Horses that are securely attached are better equipped to tolerate frustration, remain curious in the face of novelty, and adapt more fluidly to change. For example, a horse learning a new task or working in a mildly stressful situation such as in a new environment or around unfamiliar horses, will benefit from the emotional and cognitive scaffolding (Vygotsky & Luria, 1994; 2008) offered by their trusted human. When the caregiver is calm, consistent, and responsive to the horse's signals, the horse is more likely to approach learning with confidence. This emotional safety fosters optimal learning conditions and quickens the acquisition of new behaviours.

Attachment theory helps explain the behavioural resilience observed in securely attached animals. These horses often exhibit greater composure in challenging settings, such as veterinary clinics, busy urban environments, or agility rinks, because they rely on the caregiver as a source of emotional feedback and regulation. This dynamic reduces the likelihood of fear-based reactions and supports the development of robust coping mechanisms. For the trainer, recognizing and reinforcing these secure patterns can prevent or even resolve common behavioural issues rooted in anxiety, hyper-reactivity, and hyperactivity.

Attachment theory is also particularly useful when working with horses who are reactive or anxious. Many reactive behaviours like barking, lunging, and pulling are not simply the result of poor impulse control or aggression. Instead, they may signal an insecure attachment style, in which the horse lacks confidence in the caregiver's ability to manage the situation and offer positive feedback to help solve the problem. In these cases, training that focuses solely on obedience may be ineffective or even counterproductive. What the horse truly needs is a consistent, sensitive partner, someone who listens to their stress signals, creates structure, and helps them co-regulate. Through a combination of desensitization, counter conditioning, and attuned social and cognitive interaction, trainers can help reactive horses shift toward more secure attachment styles, reducing their reactivity throughout.

Incorporating attachment theory into training also means redefining the role of the trainer and caregiver. Rather than viewing the horse as a subject to be controlled, the relationship becomes one of mutual communication and trust. Ethical training methods that prioritize positive reinforcement, social learning, and emotional attunement naturally align with attachment-based principles. When caregivers respond promptly and appropriately to their horse's emotional needs, whether that means offering space, comfort, or encouragement, they model the sensitivity that Ainsworth identified as essential to secure attachment.

Attachment theory provides a powerful framework linking early-caregiver bonds to lifelong behavioural and emotional outcomes. Understanding attachment origins, from Bowlby's ethological roots to Ainsworth's SSP, enables animal trainers to shape emotionally secure relationships that enhance learning, resilience, and well-being in horses. By intentionally reinforcing secure-base behaviours and modelling sensitivity, trainers help support confident equid partners.

The following list includes behaviours I teach all the horses I work with. They prove effective at modifying insecure attachment forms to secure ones. I consider them vital for their function, form, understanding, and simplicity of execution. I train all these behaviours within two weeks. For my clients, it can take much longer.

Name → check-in	Give
Mine	Stop
Touch	Stand
What's that	Out
Backup	Ouch
Find it	Recall (whistle)
Go	Down
Take	Directed brain games

Building a SCAT Practice

Applying social cognitive animal training in everyday life involves a change in mindset as much as a change in technique. Instead of asking, *How do I get my horse to do this?* We can ask, *What would help my horse understand this? How can I teach my horse how to learn from social, cognitive, and environmental determinants?*

The practical application of SCAT does not begin with obedience cues or mechanical drills, but with the development of emotional security. Animals, like people, require safe and predictable relationships to learn meaningfully. We must become a reliable and emotionally safe presence before we ask animals to solve problems, imitate our actions, or generalize behaviours across contexts.

The first horse I trained using SCAT was a palomino quarter horse named Duck. Through imitation, Duck taught Cookie, who trained Moccasin, a haflinger cross friesian. Twenty-eight years later, I saw Dobby teach Peanut, the Wildie from Alberta, who then shared his knowledge with Sunny, a professional athlete.

Attachment theory teaches us that emotional bonds form not through dominance or control, but through consistency, responsiveness, and trust. To build secure attachment, I often start with basic behaviourist tools; not to control the animal, but to create a reliability framework. The following is a proven SCAT protocol. Before I start, I implement house rules: mine, no biting, box, exercise pen, water, and feeding areas. The station behaviour is optional, etc. There's no right or wrong house rules; they are yours to determine. Once established, consistent is key.

1. When the horse (normally a foal) arrives, if it wants to play, it does so on its own. I will pet it just a little because the horse is stressed from

the move and relocation of living quarters. It needs to decompress to avoid overstimulation. Constant interaction will keep responses high, reinforcing sensory overload, which will create problems.

2. Day one of training, I reinforce curiosity. The cue is *What's This/That*. This will remain an important cue and behaviour throughout the horse's life. During socialization, I can reinforce curiosity behaviour multiple times per day. Eventually, I will reinforce it when necessary.

3. Day two, life begins. The first thing the horse learns is its name, which establishes the check-in (look at me) without training it or asking for it. I like efficiency training.

4. The second behaviour all my horses learn is *Mine*. This behaviour prevents food stealing and biting and establishes trust. I give affection during this process; how could I resist? I make sure not to over-arouse the foal. Dopamine is addictive in a negative, undesirable way.

5. On the fourth day, I take those three simple behaviours (*name, what's this, and mine*) on the road and practice in a variety of environments. If you follow me on social media, you've seen me train this way. I work in the rink, paddock, field, or near roads; whatever environment I have access to works.

6. During the first week, I include directed brain games in our training sessions. My horses learn this via cognitive conditioning or imitation by watching the adult horse work, learning the

word *work*. It is all about efficiency.

7. Each day I plan a new adventure. I ask my horse before leaving, *Peter, are you ready for an adventure?* It helps change my frame of mind when I'm overworked but still need to train my horses. Plus, my training sessions always turn into adventures.

Daily, I spontaneously reward previously trained behaviours, adding novel ones every two to three days. These small reinforcement sessions teach the horse that its actions matter, that communication is reciprocal, and that I notice and respect its emotional expressions. I always acknowledge and verbally reward a horse's *shake* behaviour.

As the months pass, I decrease the introduction of new behaviours and adventures to about three per week, emphasizing advanced training instead. With SCAT, there's a difference between training (cognitive learning), social interaction (social learning), and environmental stimulation. Life is about satisfying all three determinants. I often have imitation sessions with the horses. We vocalize, exchange facial expressions, and physically play; yes, that means making a fool of myself.

At this stage, imitation becomes a powerful force. Animals, especially social species like horses, naturally observe the behaviour and emotional states of others in their environment. When they feel safe, they mirror our actions, sometimes subtly, sometimes directly. I nurture this tendency through simple demonstrations. By moving slowly, breathing audibly, or interacting gently with objects in the environment. With the adult horse, I offer the animal behavioural to model. These are not commands, but invitations. I cue the horse's investigation of novel stimuli with *What's That*. The horse watches, processes, and sometimes repeats the behaviour. Over time, this leads to a sense of shared rhythm and intention, what attachment researchers might call synchrony.

As the bond strengthens, you can begin introducing more complex forms of interaction, especially cognitive challenges. Here, I move from emotional safety to mental stimulation. But this is not a leap; it is a natural progression. The animal trusts the human enough to take risks, explore problems, and tolerate frustration. The animal is learning how to learn.

A few months ago, I trained an eight-month-old foal to *touch* my hand with his nose. Fast-forward three months: a new horse, Peanut, I affectionately renamed Peter Planter (PP) joined the work team. I began the *touch* process with PP to build trust, and in return, trust built our relationship. This week, Dobby, now eleven months old, showed PP, the four-year-old gelding, that affection is pleasurable. PP consented to his first, very brief, head-and-neck caress.

At Dogue Academy, I leave nothing to chance. Students and I intentionally shape the social cognitive determinants because setting the animal up for success is essential. I use and teach directed brain games to foster this process. These aren't obedience drills; they're structured opportunities for the horse to think, experiment, and succeed.

A well-designed brain game session stimulates multiple senses. I might ask a horse to locate a toy in a container, remove a lid to access food, or manipulate objects to uncover a reward. The puzzles vary in difficulty and setting. One day, the challenge might happen in the barn, the next day in the field, or even on a walk. This variety builds adaptability and generalization, while providing emotional scaffolding. The message to the animal is clear: *You are safe to try. I trust you to solve this problem. I'm here if you need support.* What emerges from this layered process is a more skilled learner and a much deeper relationship. Cognitive effort, when supported by emotional security, strengthens social bonds.

The horse grows in confidence, and the human becomes a partner in growth, not a source of pressure or control.

During my third training session with PP this week, Dobby broke away from his trainer, the fabulous Julie Langois, and the young foal walked over to check in with me. We allow these spontaneous moments because they reinforce our bonds. Dobby wanted a caress and a kiss. Satisfied, he returned to Julie. The entire exchange took just 24 seconds. I film all our sessions, so I posted it on social media; it was too cute not to.

This is where the true elegance of social cognitive animal training reveals itself, in the interplay between the social, cognitive, and environmental determinants of behaviour. These three forces do not operate in isolation. They are deeply interconnected and constantly influence one another in both directions. A secure social bond enhances the animal's ability to engage cognitively. Cognitive success reinforces the social bond by building mutual trust. A well-prepared environment supports both processes, providing the space, sensory input, and consistency to allow learning to flourish.

However, the system is fragile. If one determinant ceases to function, so do the others. An overstimulating or chaotic environment undermines emotional security and cognitive focus. A poorly structured cognitive task can lead to frustration, anxiety, or avoidance, even if the relationship is strong. Most critically, a break in social trust, whether through fear, inconsistency, or neglect, shuts down the entire system; the horse disengages, and learning stops.

Understanding the bidirectional nature of the model is essential. The determinants must maintain balance. As such, the environment needs to be adaptable, structured enough to offer clarity but flexible enough to support exploration and curiosity. We must choose the cognitive tasks with care: not too simple to bore, not too complex to frustrate. Above all, we must nurture the social relationship consistently through empathy, observation, and presence. The trainer's role is to monitor the system in real time, adjusting one element to support the others as needed. SCAT demands more than technical training skills; it requires emotional intelligence and a deep respect for the animal's inner world.

- A secure social relationship enhances the horse's willingness to try something new (social → cognitive). Trust in the human caregiver creates emotional safety, which unlocks curiosity and exploration.

- The successful completion of a cognitive challenge builds confidence, which feeds back into the bond (cognitive → social). As the horse succeeds, its trust in the human's guidance deepens, transforming their relationship into a partnership.

- A well-structured environment allows both social interaction and cognitive growth to flourish (environment → social and cognitive). When we minimize distractions and we thoughtfully arrange resources, the setting supports connection and learning.

- A calm emotional state shaped by a safe social connection allows the horse to explore the environment (social → environment). Without fear, it is free to investigate, manipulate, and engage with the world.

- Cognitive engagement transforms how the horse perceives and uses the environment (cognitive → environment). As it gains in problem-solving and decision-making skills, the horse sees the environment as full of opportunities rather than threats. Puzzles become approachable, novel situations feel navigable, and space becomes a resource for discovery rather than something to be avoided.

In this integrated model, social animals are no longer seen as passive receiver of commands or as a behaviour to be controlled. Horses become thinking, feeling, and learning individual. The goal is not compliance but cooperation, not perfection but participation. Horse training becomes a conversation, a mutual exchange between two species navigating the world together. Consent and self-efficacy lead to locus of control; the essence of a horse's umwelt.

Shifting to SCAT

Urban-dwelling horses live in environments that are radically different from their evolutionary past. They share their environment with other surrounding homes. Their emotions, and sometimes even their identity, get caught up in the chaos. Yet many training methods and learning theories still treat them as programmable machines, relying heavily on negative reinforcement or food lures. While these methods can produce behaviours, they often fail the horse's mind, emotions, or need for connection.

Social cognitive animal training offers a necessary shift. It reflects what we now know about the emotional and cognitive complexity of equids. It honours the richness of the human-animal bond and embraces training as a shared, reciprocal process rooted in communication, empathy, and mutual respect.

One of the key advantages of SCAT is that it creates consensual, resilient learners. Horses trained through observation, imitation, sensory stimulation, and social interaction aren't simply responding to a piece of food or to avoid something. They're engaged physically, mentally and emotionally. They learn how to learn. This makes them better equipped to navigate new environments, solve problems, and make effective decisions in unfamiliar situations.

SCAT also provides enhanced social harmony. When social animals feel secure, understood, and trusted, they're less likely to exhibit fearful or aggressive behaviour. Relationships become more cooperative, and everyday interactions such as grooming, veterinarian visits, or rides in busy places, become smoother and enjoyable.

Importantly, social cognitive animal training supports the ethical evolution of how we work with animals. It moves us away from control-based paradigms toward consent-based relationships. It invites us to view horses not as subjects to be managed, but as thinking, feeling beings with their perspectives, motivations, and emotional landscapes.

SCAT is Lure-free Training

Lure training originated from the principles of operant conditioning developed by B. F. Skinner in the mid-20th century, where scientists modelled behaviour with food rewards. Although Skinner didn't use food lures himself, his work laid the foundation for reward-based animal training. Veterinary behaviourists like Ian Dunbar and trainer Karen Pryor pioneered and popularized luring in the 1980s and 1990s.

Dunbar and Pryor adapted techniques first refined in marine mammal training, where force was not an option, to domestic horses, using food as a guide to elicit behaviours like come, stand still, and load. Lure training quickly became a staple of positive reinforcement methods because it allowed trainers and pet owners to produce fast, visible results without physical coercion. However, the approach relies on the prompt, cue, and reward as a single piece of information, which leads to confusion.

In traditional training, lures, usually food, are used to guide animals into behaviours. While this seems harmless, and often effective in the short term, overuse of lures hinders deeper learning, becoming a crutch. Lures keep the animal focused on the reward, not the interaction or the task itself. This creates dependency rather than understanding. The horse may comply only when the food is visible, or worse, become confused or anxious when the lure disappears.

Lure-free training demands more from the human. It asks us to communicate clearly, model behaviour, and build trust. But it also demands more from the animal, in the best possible way. Training without lures requires the animal to think, interpret, and engage. Thinking is where real learning lives and where relationships flourish.

Another downside to lure training is that horse trainers and caregivers will have to fade the food and cue associated with it (closed hand or pinched fingers). Because of the horse's emotional dependence on the lure, it makes the procedure difficult. The process of fading lures and cues takes time. Why add lures when they'll need to be removed? In my professional experience, there's no need to add unnecessary steps. Horse training is about efficiency.

In exotic animal training, the use of lures is dangerous. Food bribes have no effect on a caged animal who can be wherever it wants to be. Starving animals to use lures is unethical and potentially life-threatening. I would never use lures to train wolves; a fancy living too much. By avoiding food bribes, we shift from transactional exchanges to relational teaching, saving time. The horse is not performing a trick for a treat; it is sharing an experience, fostering independence, self-control, and emotional stability.

SCAT Builds Resilience

Resilience is the ability to recover from stress, adapt to change, and move forward with emotional balance. In horses, just like in humans, resilience is modifiable; we can cultivate it through thoughtful, relationship-based training. In a social cognitive framework, resilience is not an outcome of repetition or obedience, but the result of a secure attachment.

Resilient learners begin with a solid social foundation. When a horse feels securely attached to a person, it gains the emotional confidence to take risks, make mistakes, and try again. Frustration is not the enemy; it becomes part of learning. The key is to introduce frustration in measured doses, in ways the horse can handle it. Rather than overwhelming or pressuring them, we offer gentle cognitive challenges that stretch their problem-solving abilities. For example, presenting a horse with a puzzle that is just beyond its current skill level, such as a directed brain game, invites them to struggle briefly, then succeed. Through this success, the horse learns that persistence pays off, and over time, its tolerance for difficulty grows.

Directed brain games also create an association between the human and the horse, creating a secure attachment. The SCAT trainer then transfers the problem-solving feedback loop to real-life situations. Instead of constantly being hypervigilant during walks, the horse asks the person for information. Horses who learned the *touch* behaviour will engage a distracted handler, requesting their guidance. The spaces in which learning happens matter. Enriched environments filled with various stimuli allow horses to explore, make choices, and recover from stressors. These controlled challenges build resilience without forcing it.

Resilience grows when animals can think. Encouraging decision-making, no matter how small, helps horses build a sense of control over their experience. Whether choosing between two puzzles, determining when to approach, or deciding how to navigate a new location, equids who are cognitively engaged are less likely to shut down under pressure. They've practised thinking their way through challenges and know they have some agency.

Social cognitive trained horses aren't fearless or perfect, far from it. They are, however, emotionally equipped and curious about experiencing the unknown. There's no reason for them to perform behaviours on cue for the sake of a food reward because they will eat regardless of treat training. Horses aspire to live their best life by building long-lasting partnerships with humans.

Resilience training prepares our horses for life amongst people; a world unfamiliar to their natural niche. Resilience is not just something we hope horses have. It's something we help them build. Over the years, I've developed a model to reinforce psychological strength. I used it daily and teach it to animal behaviour students and horse owners alike. The following is a glimpse into how we train resilience using the

SCAT approach. This model operates on the premise that all three determinants are functional.

Your horse needs SPACE to build resilience.

The best way to understand the social cognitive animal training model is by thinking your horse needs SPACE. Social affiliation builds a positive outcomes expectancy because the horse learns it has control over when to imitate another horse, animal, or person. Positive outcome expectancy establishes locus of control and consent, which leads to a secure attachment. The emotional connection enhances cognitive training exercises performed in stressed-controlled environments. Problem-solving and making effective decisions in various settings further develops the horse's social affiliation. Resilience is the product of SPACE.

Resilience training is not a new concept. People who work in highly stressful jobs, like doctors or EMTs, must learn to tolerate high levels of stress. Psychologist and life coaches also employ resilience training techniques with their clients. As professional horse trainers and behaviour consultants, it is our duty to step away from lure-based training and instil resilience through SCAT.

Conclusion

Social cognitive animal training is more than a method; it is a relationship-centred philosophy that sees animals as thinking, feeling, and socially motivated beings. Unlike behaviourism, which often reduces learning to external reinforcement and observable outcomes, the social cognitive approach recognizes that behaviour arises from within. Emotions, relationships, expectations, and perceptions all shape how animals learn. When we ignore these internal processes, we risk suppressing behaviours without ever addressing their root cause.

By grounding our training in secure attachment, we offer animals the emotional safety they need to become active participants in their learning. Through imitation and observation, we allow social animal species to explore our intentions and mirror our actions, building trust not through control, but through mutual understanding. As we introduce cognitive challenges, whether through structured brain games, problem-solving tasks, or real-world scenarios, horses learn how to think, not just react. With each success, their confidence grows, and so does our attachment.

The environment too plays a critical role. Thoughtful and responsive settings encourage curiosity, exploration, communication, and collaboration. The social, cognitive, and environmental determinants don't operate independently. They influence each other in a bidirectional and reciprocal process, forming a dynamic learning system. A break in one determinant disrupts the whole; balance fosters resilience and growth.

When we train through an integrated lens, we invite the horse to be our partner, not our subject. We stop asking, *How do I make my horse obey?* and instead wonder, *What does my horse understand? What does it feel? How does it feel? What does it need from me right now? How can my horse thrive?* or *How does my horse perceive its life?*

The goal is to offer social animals a safe SPACE: social, positive outcome expectancy, attachment, cognitive, and environmental opportunities to learn and grow. When we consider the entire animal, not just its behaviour, we can transform undesirable behaviours into functional actions. We can alter a horse's destructive habits into strengths. Hyperactivity becomes an intellectual and physical outlet in which horses can solve complex problems, like finding an intervention entry point during a therapy session.

This shift from behaviourism and constant luring to a fully holistic training approach is profound. It changes how we train, but also how we live, work, and connect with the horses in our care. With the SCAT model, learning transforms from a unilateral command system to a shared experience; a dance between minds, guided by trust, shaped by thought, and anchored in compassion.

I invite you to join a truly remarkable revolution in horse training. Let's change our trade from punitive to masterful. We have the knowledge to engineer brains using cognition. We know how to build neural pathways to create fully functional mental, physical, and emotional non-human individuals. My question to you is, why stay stuck in the past when the future offers so much?

Choice is not a training tool. It's the condition under which learning becomes possible.

Horse Training Definitions

Behaviourism-Based Terms
Bridge: An auditory, visual, or tactile stimulus that links the reinforcement to the reward. Also known as a conditioned stimulus. Ex.: clicker, whistle, or the word *Yes!*

Classical Conditioning: Classical conditioning is a type of learning in which an organism comes to associate a neutral stimulus with a meaningful one, eventually responding to the neutral stimulus as if it were the meaningful one.

Conditioned Emotional Response: The result of pairing a stimulus with an emotional response.

Conditioned Stimulus: A previously neutral stimulus paired with a basic need, such as food, water, affection, play, etc.

Counter Conditioning: Changing a horse's emotional response to a stimulus (e.g., pairing a scary sound with treats).

Extinction: The process of reducing a behaviour by no longer reinforcing it (e.g., ignoring barking for attention).

Generalization: A horse's ability to apply learned behaviours in different environments.

Learned Helplessness: A phenomenon in which repeated exposure to stressors results in individuals inability to regulate, react, or respond.

Negative Punishment (P-): Removing a desirable stimulus to decrease a behaviour (e.g., turning away when a horse jumps for attention).

Negative Reinforcement (R-): Removing an aversive stimulus to increase a behaviour (e.g., releasing leash pressure when a horse sits).

Operant Conditioning: Operant conditioning is a type of learning in which behaviour is shaped and maintained by its consequences. Behaviours followed by reinforcement will increase in frequency, while those followed by punishment will decrease.

Positive Punishment (P+): Adding an aversive stimulus to decrease a behaviour (e.g., using a loud noise to stop jumping).

Positive Reinforcement (R+): Adding a desirable stimulus to increase a behaviour (e.g., giving a treat for sitting).

Social Cognitive Learning Terms

Agency: The concept that people have the ability to initiate and control their actions, and the feeling they experience when being in charge of their actions.

Ambivalent Attachment: A horse feels anxious and confusion by the inconsistent responses of the human caregiver.

Attachment: The result of the bonding process during the critical phase of social development in social species.

Avoidant Attachment: A horse feels uncomfortable with the human caregiver present and avoids physical contact.

Disorganized Attachment: An inconsistent, hard to predict behaviour. This bond, or lack there of, is sometimes called fearful-avoidant attachment style.

Facilitation: The presence of another horse performing a behaviour increases the likelihood the learner horse will try to perform it.

Imitation Learning: Horses can learn by watching other horses perform a behaviour.

Learner-horse: A novice horse that socially references the teacher-horse and mimics its behaviour.

Locus of Control: Refers to the degree to which an animal, or person, believes they have influence over what happens to them.

Observational Learning: Horses learn by watching and imitating people.

Secure Attachment: A horse feels confident and reassured by the presence of their human caregiver.

Self-Efficacy: One's confidence in the ability to control one's motivation, behaviour, performance and social environment.

Social Referencing: A horse looks to a trusted figure (human or equid) to determine how to respond to a new situation.

Teacher-horse: A horse that consistently performs trained behaviours at a high level, aka bomb-proofed.

Umwelt: The world as it is experienced by the experiencer, or organism.

Vicarious experience: Learning that happens by watching someone else go through an experience, rather than doing it firsthand.

Training and Definitions

Cue: A visual, auditory, or verbal command that trigger the horse to perform the behaviour.

Bomb-Proof: A horse that reliably performs behaviour at a 100% rate in every environment.

Capturing: Reinforcing a naturally occurring behaviour without prompting.

Clicker: A small metal block with a metal blade that *clicks* when pressed with the thumb. Also known as an auditory bridge or conditioned stimulus. Bridging the reinforcement to the reward.

Clicker Training: A form of marker training that uses a distinct clicking sound to indicate the exact moment a horse performs the desired behaviour, followed by a reward to reinforce the action.

Cue: A visual, auditory, or verbal command that trigger the horse to perform the behaviour.

Cue Discrimination: Teaching a horse to respond correctly to different verbal or visual cues.

Fading: Gradually reducing reliance on prompts, cues,

or reinforcers.

Flooding: A technique in which the organism is exposed directly to a maximum-intensity stimulus without any attempt made to lessen the emotional response.

Fluency: The horse's ability to perform a behaviour accurately and quickly in different environments.

Habituation: The process of repeatedly exposing the organism to a stimulus to a response.

Husbandry: The caring and breeding of captive domestic or exotic animals.

Jackpot: A jackpot is a small handful of food or treats. It can also be a larger piece of food.

Latency: The time it takes for a horse to respond to a cue.

Luring: Using a treat or object to guide a horse into position (not used in this method).

Memory Consolidation: The process by which the brain transforms temporary information into a more stable, long-lasting form during sleep.

Parkour: Urban horse agility based on military training.

Polymorphous: Environments occurring in several different forms or stages of development.

Prefrontal Cortex: The part of the brain behind the forehead is one of the last parts to mature. This area is responsible for skills like planning, prioritizing, and making good decisions.

Prompting: Using verbal, visual, or physical cues to encourage a behaviour. Prompts serve as reminders to perform a behaviour.

Proofing: Strengthening a behaviour by practicing in various settings with different distractions. Also known as bomb-proofed behaviour.

Rewards: Whatever the horse wants: food, water, rest, safety, affection, or play. Keep in mind desired rewards constantly change.

Session: A 5-minute-long horse training period.

Shaping: Reinforcing successive approximations (baby steps) toward a desired behaviour.

Stimulus: A *thing* that rouses senses, activity, or energy in an organism.

Systematic Desensitization: The incremental exposure to a stimulus without triggering the associated response.

Target: An object the animal must touch with its nose or other body part. A real human hand is also a target the horse must touch.

Testing Behaviour: Take 10 rewards to test 10 behaviours.

Testing Cues: Take 10 rewards to test 10 cues.

Transduction: The process of converting external stimuli (light, sound, pressure, scent, and taste) into electrical or chemical signals that can be interpreted by the nervous system.

Yes: An alternative sound that replaces the clicker, a conditioned stimulus: a bridge between behaviour and reward.

References

Ainsworth, M.S. (1979). Infant-mother attachment. *American Psychologist, 34*(10), 932-937. https://doi.org/10.1037/0003-066X.34.10.932

———. (1991). Attachment and other affectional bonds across the life cycle. In C.M. Parkes, J. Stevenson-Hinde, & P. Marris (Eds.). *Attachment across the life cycle,* 33-51. Routledge.

Ainsworth, M.D.S., Blehar, M.C., Waters, E., & Wall, S. (1978). *Patterns of attachment: Assessed in the strange situation and at home.* Erlbaum.

Ainsworth, M.S. & Witting, B.A. (1969). Attachment and the exploratory behaviour of one-year-olds in a strange situation. *Determinants of Infant Behaviour, 4*(4), 113-136.

American Psychological Association. (2019). *When working with animals can hurt your mental health.* Science Daily. Retrieved from www.sciencedaily.com/releases/2019/08/190809113026.htm

Arrazola, A., & Merkies, K. (2020). Effect of Human Attachment Style on Horse Behaviour and Physiology during Equine-Assisted Activities–A Pilot Study. *Animals, 10*(7), 1156. https://doi.org/10.3390/ani10071156

Bandura, A. (1965). Influence of models' reinforcement contingencies on the acquisition of imitative responses. *Journal of Personality and Social Psychology, 1*(6), 589-595. https://doi.org/10.1037/h0022070

———. (1977). Self-efficacy: Toward a unifying theory of behavioural change. *Psychological Review, 84*(2), 191-215. https://doi.org/10.1037/0033-295X.84.2.191

———. (1977). *Social learning theory.* Prentice-Hall.

———. (1982). Self-efficacy mechanism in human agency. *American Psychologist, 37*(2), 122-147.

———. (1986). *Social foundations of thought and action: A social cognitive theory.* Prentice-Hall.

———. (1989). Social cognitive theory. In R. Vasta (Ed.). Annals of child development. Vol. 6. *Six theories of child development*, 1-60. JAI Press.

———. (2001). Social Cognitive Theory: An Agentic Perspective. *Annual Review of Psychology, 52*(1), 1-60. https://doi.org/10.1146/annurev.psych.52.1.1

Bandura, A., Ross, D., & Ross, S.A. (1961). Transmission of aggression through imitation of aggressive models. *The Journal of Abnormal and Social Psychology, 63*(3), 575-582. https://doi.org/10.1037/h0045925

Berridge, K.C. (2003). Pleasures of the brain. *Brain and Cognition, 2626*(3), 1-23. https://doi.org/10.1016/S0278-2626(03)00014-9

Bowlby, J. (1969). *Attachment and loss, Vol. 1: Attachment.* Basic Books.

———. (1973). *Attachment and loss, Vol. 2: Separation.* Basic Books.

———. (l980). *Attachment and loss, Vol. 3: Loss, sadness and depression.* Basic Books.

———. (1988a). *A Secure Base: Clinical Applications of Attachment Theory.* Routledge.

———. (1988b). *A secure base: Parent-child attachment and healthy human development.* Routledge.

Bowlby, J., & Ainsworth, M. (1991). An ethological approach to personality development. *American Psychologist, 46*(4), 333-341.

Bretherton, I. (1992). The Origins of Attachment Theory: John Bowlby and Mary Ainsworth. *Developmental Psychology, 28,* 759-775. https://doi.org/10.1037/0012-1649.28.5.759.

Brown, J.S., Collins, A., & Duguid, P. (1989). Situated cognition and the culture of learning. *Educational Researcher, 18*(1), 32-42.

Buccino, G., Binkofski, F., & Riggio, L. (2004). The mirror neuron system and action recognition. *Brain and Language, 89*(2), 370-376. https://doi.org/10.1016/S0093-934X(03)00356-0

DeAraugo, J., McLean, A., McLaren, S., Caspar, G., McLean, M., & McGreevy, P. (2014). Training methodologies differ with theattachment of humans to horses. *Journal of Veterinary Behavior: Clinical Applications and Research, 9*(5), 235–241. https://doi.org/10.1016/j.jveb.2014.05.001

Duranton, C., & Gaunet, F. (2018). Behavioural synchronization and affiliation: Horses exhibit human-like skills. *Learning & Behaviour, 46*(4), 364-373. https://doi.org/10.3758/s13420-018-0323-4

Durning, S.J., & Artino, A.R. (2011). Situativity theory: a perspective on how participants and the environment can interact: AMEE Guide no. 52. *Medical Teacher, 33*(3), 188-99. https://doi.org/10.3109/0142159X.2011.550965. PMID: 21345059.

Fugazza, C., & Higaki, F. (2024). *Do As I Do 2nd Edition: Using Social Learning to Train Horses.* Horsewise.

Gallese, V., Fadiga, L., Fogassi, L., & Rizzolatti G. (1996). Action recognition in the premotor cortex. *Brain, 119*(2), 593-609. https://doi.org/10.1093/brain/119.2.593. PMID: 8800951

Hanggi, E.B. (2010). Short-term Memory Testing in Domestic Horses: Experimental Design Plays a Role. *Journal of Equine Veterinary Science, 30*(11), 617-623, ISSN 0737-0806. https://doi.org/10.1016/j.jevs.2010.10.004.

Harlow, H.F., Dodsworth, R.O., & Harlow, M.K. (1965). Total social isolation in monkeys. *Proceedings of the National Academy of Sciences of the United States of America, 54*(1), 90.

Harlow, H.F., & Zimmermann, R.R. (1958). The development of affective responsiveness in infant monkeys. *Proceedings of the American Philosophical Society, 102,* 501-509.

Hartmann, E., Rehn, T., Christensen, J. W., Nielsen, P. P., & McGreevy, P. (2021). From the Horse's Perspective: Investigating Attachment Behaviour and the Effect of Training Method on Fear Reactions and Ease of Handling-A Pilot Study. *Animals : an open access journal from MDPI, 11*(2), 457. https://doi.org/10.3390/ani11020457

Henderson, A. (2024). What's love got to do with it? Exploring the horse to human attachment bond. *Concordia International Equestrian Magazine.* Retrieved from https://www.researchgate.net/publication/385746506_What's_love_got_to_do_with_it_Exploring_the_horse_to_human_attachment_bond

Henry, S., Richard-Yris, M. A., & Hausberger, M. (2006). Influence of various early human-foal interferences on subsequent human-foal relationship. *Developmental psychobiology, 48*(8), 712–718. https://doi.org/10.1002/dev.20189

Henry, S., Richard-Yris, M.-A., Tordjman, S., & Hausberger, M. (2009). Neonatal handling affects durably bonding and social development. *PLOS ONE, 4,* e5216. https://doi.org/10.1371/journal.pone.0005216

Ijichi, C., Griffin, K., Squibb, K., & Favier, R., (2018). Stranger danger? An investigation into the influence of human-horse bond on stress and behaviour. *Applied Animal Behaviour Science, 206,*

59-63, ISSN 0168-1591.
https://doi.org/10.1016/j.applanim.2018.05.034.
Jackson, J. (2013). *Paddock Paradise: A Guide to Natural Horse Boarding*. Star Ridge Publishing.
Kaufman, C.J., & Kaufman, A.B. (2004). Applying a creativity framework to animal cognition. *New Ideas in Psychology 22*, 143-155.
https://doi.org/10.1016/j.newideapsych.2004.09.006
Kilner, J.M., & Lemon, R.N. (2013). What we know currently about mirror neurons. *Current biology, 23*(23), 1057-1062.
https://doi.org/10.1016/j.cub.2013.10.051
Lave, J. (1988). *Cognition in practice: Mind, mathematics, and culture in everyday life*. Cambridge University Press.
Lave, J., & Wenger, E. (1990). *Situated Learning: Legitimate Peripheral Participation*. Cambridge University Press.
LeDoux, J.E. (2000). Emotion circuits in the brain. *Annual Review of Neuroscience, 23*(1), 155-184.
https://doi.org/10.1146/annurev.neuro.23.1.155
Lorenz, K. (1937). On the formation of the concept of instinct. *Natural Sciences, 25*(19), 289-300.
https://doi.org/10.1007/BF01492648
———. (1965). *Evolution and modification of behaviour*. University of Chicago Press.
———. (1966). *On Aggression*. Harcourt, Brace & World.
———. (1981). *The Year of the Greylag Goose*. Methuen Publishing Ltd.
———. (2002). *Man Meets Horse*. Routledge Classics.
———. (2002). *King Solomon's Ring (2nd ed.)*. Routledge.
Mahn, H. (1999). Vygotsky's methodological contribution to sociocultural theory. *Remedial and Special Education, 20*(6), 341-350. ISSN: 0741-9325

Mcleod, S. (2025). Vygotsky's Theory of Cognitive Development. Simply Psychology. https://doi.org/10.5281/zenodo.15680745

Molenberghs, P., Cunnington, R., & Mattingley, J.B. (2009). Is the mirror neuron system involved in imitation? A short review and meta-analysis. *Neuroscience and Biobehavioral Reviews, 33*(7), 975-980. https://doi.org/10.1016/j.neubiorev.2009.03.010

Nagasawa, M., Mogi, K., & Kikusui, T. (2009). Attachment between humans and horses. *Japanese Psychological Research, 51*(3), 209-221. https://doi.org/10.1111/j.1468-5884.2009.00402.x

Nagasawa, M., Kawai, E., Mogi, K., & Kikusui, T. (2013). Horses show left facial lateralization upon reunion with their owners. *Behavioural Processes, 98,* 112-116. https://doi.org/10.1016/j.beproc.2013.05.012

Owen, S. (2004). *Situativity theory and emerging trends in teacher professional development.* Australian Association for Research in Education (AARE). http://www.aare.edu.au/data/publications/2004/owe04331.pdf

Pasqualotto, R., Löhr, S., & Stoltz, T. (2015). Skinner and Vygotsky's Understanding of Resilience in the School Environment. *Creative Education, 6,* 1841-1851. https://doi.org/10.4236/ce.2015.617188

Payne, E., DeAraugo, J., Bennett, P., & McGreevy, P. (2016). Exploring the existence and potential underpinnings of dog-human and horse-human attachment bonds. *Behavioural processes, 125,* 114–121. https://doi.org/10.1016/j.beproc.2015.10.004

Pfungst, O. (1911). *Clever Hans (The horse of Mr. von Osten): A contribution to experimental animal and human psychology (Trans. C.L. Rahn).* Henry Holt.

Premack, D. (1959). Toward empirical behaviour laws: I. Positive reinforcement. *Psychology Review, 66*(4), 21-233.

———. (1963). Rate differential reinforcement in monkey manipulation. *Journal of the Experimental Analysis of Behaviour, 6*(1), 81-89. https://doi.org/10.1901/jeab.1963.6-81

Reesor, L.V.E. (2017). Addressing Outcomes Expectancies in Behaviour Change. *American Journal of Lifestyle Medicine, 11*(6), 430-432. https://doi.org/10.1177/1559827617722504.

Rehn, T., McGowan, R.T., & Keeling, L.J. (2013). Evaluating the Strange Situation Procedure (SSP) to assess the bond between horses and humans. *PloS one, 8*(2), e56938. https://doi.org/10.1371/journal.pone.0056938

Richard, W., & Burkhardt, J. (2005). *Patterns of Behaviour Konrad Lorenz, Niko Tinbergen, and the Founding of Ethology*. Chicago Press.

Rizzolatti, G., Fadiga, L., Gallese, V., & Fogassi, L. (1996). Premotor cortex and the recognition of motor actions. Brain research. *Cognitive Brain Research, 3*(2), 131-141. https://doi.org/10.1016/0926-6410(95)00038-0

Rizzolatti, G., & Craighero, L. (2004). The mirror-neuron system. *Annual Review of Neuroscience, 27*(1), 169-192. https://doi.org/10.1146/annurev.neuro.27.070203.144230

Rizzolatti, G. (2005). The mirror neuron system and its function in humans. *Anatomy and Embryology, 210*(5-6), 419-421. https://doi.org/10.1007/s00429-005-0039-z

Rizzolatti, G., & Fabbri-Destro, M. (2008). The mirror system and its role in social cognition. *Current Opinion in Neurobiology, 18*(2), 179-184. https://doi.org/10.1016/j.conb.2008.08.001

Salamone, J.D., & Correa, M. (2012). The Mysterious Motivational Functions of Mesolimbic Dopamine.

Neuron, 76(3), 470-485.
https://doi.org/10.1016/j.neuron.2012.10.021

Sapolsky, R.M. (2017). *Behave: the biology of humans at our best and worst*. Penguin Press.

Schultz, W. (2007). Behavioural dopamine signals. *Trends in Neurosciences, 30*(5), 203-210.
https://doi.org/10.1016/j.tins.2007.03.007

———. (2004). Neural coding of basic reward terms of animal learning theory, game theory, microeconomics and behavioural ecology. *Current Opinion in Neurobiology, 14*, 139-147.
https://doi.org/10.1016/j.conb.2004.03.017

Scott, J.P. (1958). Critical Periods in the Development of Social Behaviour in Puppies. *Psychosomatic Medicine, 20*(1), 43-54.

Scott, J.P., & Fuller, J.L. (1965). *Genetics and the Social Behaviour of the Horse*. University of Chicago Press.

Shinkaruk, K., Carr, E., Lockyer, J., & Hecker, K. (2022). Exploring the development of interprofessional competence and professional identity: A Situated Learning Theory study. *Journal of Interprofessional Care, 37*, 1-10.
https://doi.org/10.1080/13561820.2022.2140129.

Skinner, E.A. (1996). A guide to constructs of control. *Journal of Personality and Social Psychology, 71*(3), 549-570. https://doi.org/10.1037/0022-3514.71.3.549

Solomon, J., Beetz, A., Schöberl, I., Gee, N., & Kotrschal, K. (2019). Attachment security in companion horses: adaptation of Ainsworth's strange situation and classification procedures to horses and their human caregivers. *Attachment & human development, 21*(4), 389-417.
https://doi.org/10.1080/14616734.2018.1517812

Sutton, J. (2025). Mirror Neurons and the Neuroscience of Empathy. Retrieved from Positive psychology https://positivepsychology.com/mirror-neurons/

Tinbergen, N. (1951). The Study of Instinct. Oxford University Press.

———. (1953). *Social behaviour in animals: With special reference to vertebrates*. Methuen.

———. (1969). *The Study of Instinct*. Clarendon Press.

Teglas, E., Gergely, A., Kupan, K., Miklósi, A., & Topál, J. (2012). Horses' Gaze Following Is Tuned to Human Communicative Signals. *Current Biology, 22*(3), 209-212. https://doi.org/10.1016/j.cub.2011.12.018

Topál, J., Miklósi, A., Csányi, V., & Dóka, A. (1998). Attachment Behaviour in Horses (Canis familiaris): A New Application of Ainsworth's (1969) Strange Situation Test. *Journal of Comparative Psychology, 112*(3), 219-229. https://doi.org/10.1037/0735-7036.112.3.219

Vygotsky, L.S. (1980). *Mind in Society: Development of Higher Psychological Processes*. Harvard University Press. ISBN 9780674576292

Vygotsky, L.S., & Luria, A. (1994). *Tool and Symbol in Child Development. In R. Van Der Veer, & J. Valsiner (Eds.), The Vygotsky Reader*. Blackwell Publishers.

Vygotsky, L.S., & Luria, A. (2008). Tool and symbol in child development. ID: 11433655 https://doi.org/10.2307/j.ctvjf9vz4.6Corpus

What is Situated Cognition. (2022). Retrieved 21 February 2022, from IGI Global. https://www.igi-global.com/dictionary/designing-automated-learning-effective-training/27047

Author Biography

Gaby Dufresne-Cyr is a distinguished horse trainer and accomplished author with a deep understanding of exotic animal behaviour and training. Her passions include sharing her knowledge with others. Her books cover a wide range of topics, from basic training and behaviour modification to advanced concepts in psychology and communication. Despite grappling with dyslexia, Gaby has harboured a profound passion for writing from an early age. In her twenties, she contributed to the French periodical Passionnement Chien for four years before venturing into the digital realm with her blogs aimed at assisting individuals. Gaby authored the following books.

- *An Introduction to Social Cognitive Animal Training: The Evolution of Dog Training* (2025)
- *Beyond the Lure: How to Train Dogs* series. (2025)
- *Animal-Assisted Therapy: Superstars Change Teen Lives.* (2024)
- *Horse in the Mirror is God: A Scientifically Spiritual Approach to Treating Human and Animal Behaviour Problems.* (2018)

www.gabydufresnecyr.com
www.dogueacademy.com

www.ingramcontent.com/pod-product-compliance
Lightning Source LLC
Chambersburg PA
CBHW042341150426
43196CB00001B/14